STREET MACHINES

Andrew Morland

STREET MACHINES

'49 AND ON CUSTOM CARS

Osprey Colour Series

Published in 1984 by Osprey Publishing Limited
12–14 Long Acre, London WC2E 9LP
Member Company of the George Philip Group

British Library Cataloguing in Publication Data
Morland, Andrew
   Street machines.—(Osprey colour series)
   I. Automobiles—Customizing—Pictorial works
   I. Title
   629.2'222   TL154
ISBN 0-85045-546-4

Captions and text by Colin Burnham
Editor Tim Parker

Printed in Hong Kong

The dictionary defines a 'machine' as *apparatus in which the action of several parts is combined for the applying of mechanical force to a purpose*. Most folk use some form of street 'apparatus'. In the majority of cases, it's sole purpose is that of daily transportation, and little thought is spared for those parts that provide the all-important motive force. A street machiner on the other hand, like any auto hobbyist, views his machine in a different light to most. It is more personal than any mass-produced 'daily driver' could ever be. If he feels that any aspect of it could be improved upon or changed for the better, especially in terms of performance, he will take the time to do it. It's his pride and joy; a hand-crafted representation of his imagination, skill and individual taste. As such it will more than likely contain a whole host of trick features and components which, collectively, add up to a much more exciting piece of apparatus than the original. And, while every street machiner enjoys the on-going process of actually modifying his machine, *nuthin'* beats driving it on the street.

Officially, a 'street machine' is *any modified street-driven vehicle of 1949 or later manufacture*. Theoretically, this should include fifties-style customs, California lowriders,

and various other American automotive sub-cultures. But in practice, the term is applied to late-model hot rods; the muscle-bound Chevies, Fords and Mopars that have been roaming the boulevards *lookin' bad* for nearly a quarter-century. It is a movement that has its roots firmly implanted in the dragstrip and largely comprises the supercars or 'factory hot rods' of yesteryear, often totally rebuilt to emulate stock-bodied race cars. Of course, as with any 'street' culture, the accepted image has changed much over the years; from the jacked-up no-nonsense grey primer look of the early sixties, to the contemporary nose-down stance with wall-to-wall rubber tucked under the back and fine 'detailing' in every department. However, as the photographs in this book show, the street machine movement encompasses a myriad of different treatments, body styles and, moreover, personalities behind them. Most were shot at the 1983 *Car Craft* Magazine Street Machine Nationals in Springfield, Illinois, an annual harvest of horsepower that attracts enthusiasts from every corner of the United States. In short, the name of the game is 'Show'n'Go'. Enjoy it.

Colin Burnham Pinner, Middlesex

Andrew Morland is a freelance photographer whose automotive work appears regularly in various European enthusiast publications. *STREET MACHINES* is his fourth book in the Osprey Colour Series; following *OFF ROAD*, *STREET RODS* and *CUSTOM MOTORCYCLES*. He lives with his wife and daughter (and a collection of old and not so old cars and bikes) in a small village near Glastonbury in Somerset.

No book of this type could have been published without a lot of co-operation from a lot of people, particularly those who actually exhibited their custom work. Both photographer and publisher salute those people. Special thanks must go to the organizers of the Street Machine Nationals in Springfield, Illinois in 1983 who simply made things easy. Also to Ian Harbottle who came along for the ride, made the notes and provided encouragement. Who said photography was nothing but work?

Contents

'Glass is class— when it's Corvette shaped

One of the most outstanding street machines at the 1983 *Car Craft* Nationals was Rick Dyer's Pro Street Vette. From its flawless Candy Brandywine paint to its fully-detailed 454-in. powerplant, this fine '59 represents the very best in Corvettes *and* 'Pro-Street'—the state-of-the-art street—legal race car movement in America. A beautiful specimen indeed

Rick never misses an opportunity to 'light-up' those gigantic Goodyears—especially when there's a photographer around

Below When the owner decides to let loose the power, boy does this thing move!

Left The front end is removable for easy access to the and suspension. The overbored early 454 'rat' is fitted engine with TRW 12.5-to-1 pistons, hi-po Chevy rods, a Reed mushroom tappet cam, Manley valves, Crane roller rockers and valve springs, and worked-on aluminium D-port open chamber heads. The block was machined and tricked-up by *Shadow Woods Racing* of Mt Clemens, Michigan (Rick's home town), then topped with a fully polished Crower fuel-injection system. A Turbo 400 trans with 5500 rpm stall Fairbanks converter and Auto Stick III shifter harnesses the abundant torque, and transfers it to a narrowed 5.57-geared Chrysler Dana (spooled) rear end outfitted with Summers Bros. axles.

The latter rides on coil-over/4-link suspension, while front suspension is original '59 Corvette. The chassis is also original, although the rear frame rails were moved inboard to clear the 15 × 33 in. slicks

Left There's the man himself, 35 year old Rick Dyer. Corvette buffs will notice that the original tooth-design '59 grille has been swapped for a plain black '62 item

Below Red anodized ram pipes on the fuel-injection make a pretty picture. Virtually everything under the (non-existent) hood has been fastidiously polished or chrome plated

Below A 15 gallon fuel tank was custom built to fit between the wheeltubs, while a heavy-duty truck battery resides beneath that louvred ally cover. Again, both are polished to perfection. 40-in. wheelie bars assure things don't get too carried away when Rick puts the pedal to the metal

Right The nose-down Vette is capable of running the standing quarter-mile in 9.46 seconds at 142 mph—plenty quick for a street licensed vehicle

Left Al Woodward is president of the V8 Estate Corvette Club in his home town of Detroit, so it's only fitting he should have the snazziest, most power packin' car in the city. This '72 Vette is the proverbial *kandy-kolored tangerine-flake streamline baby*, with as much 'go' as 'show'. When he and his wife Elizabeth—the Glass Roots Racing Team—aren't doing their thing at the local dragstrip, you can be sure they're winning admiring looks on the street

Above Under (and largely through) the hood lies the biggest, brightest, blown big block imaginable. The motor began as a 454 Chevy, and has been treated to an $\frac{1}{8}$ in. overbore and a $\frac{5}{8}$ in. stroker crank, which brings the capacity up to an incredible 543 cubic inches! And it's not just big muscle, but strong muscle too, with polished and ported heads, a roller cam, Accel distributor, and dual 660 double pumpers. Without the 6-71 blower, Al clocked 178.60 mph on the Bonneville salt flats, and with it his wife Elizabeth turns regular 10-second quarter-miles on the strip. Because the engine has a blower and a high compression ratio, low-octane pump gas is useless. Consequently Al brews his own, based on aviation gas, with additions of tolvene, benzol, and a gallon of Moroso Octane Booster per tankful

Overleaf They say that street machines reflect their owner's personality. If the Woodward Corvette is anything to go by, then it's certainly true

17

Above Yosemite Sam, a Motown painter of national repute, demonstrated virtually *every* custom paint technique on this multi-colored machine. The butterfly wings and some of the striping are picked out in real gold leaf, the rest is a mixture of candies and pearls

Left Woodward's cockpit was re-trimmed by H & H Interiors of Detroit in black and gold velvet. The dash plaques denote some of the more memorable race meetings and shows the team has participated in

From front or rear this stunning Corvette is like no other. All the suspension has been fully chromed, the wheelwells have anodized aluminum liners and there's also a full ally belly pan punched with 88 louvres for engine and trans cooling

Overleaf A shimmering Metalflake paint scheme makes this '69 Stingray stand out from the crowd, albeit 'out of style'

Right William Edward Wright of Delaware, Ohio, owns this Candy Red '58. Apart from the paint and wheels, the only thing that distinguishes it from a stocker is the hi-rise carburation set-up poking through the hood. Originally it had a row of phoney louvres in the same location

Far right The stock 290-horse 283 has been replaced by a clean 402-incher out of a '69 Chevelle. Naturally it was given the 'once-over' before the Weiand intake and dual 650 Holleys were bolted on

Below Those overly-bold chrome strips on the '58 decklid were intended to match the 'bulk' of the front end, but were discarded in '59 along with the pseudo hood louvres. Steve Easter sprayed the Candy Red paint over a Trans Am Gold base color

'C'mon man, I've gotta driver's licence . . .'.
Classic Corvette is strictly for business

In 1958, General Motors chief stylist, Bill Mitchell, designed a few odd-ball Corvettes to demonstrate new ideas for the future and provide vehicles for a travelling roadshow staged by GM. One of them, the XP-700, had a swoopy, goldfish-like front end, and a rear which found its way on to the '61 Vette. What you see here is not the actual XP-700, but a '60 Corvette with a replica front end—a regular purist's nightmare! Put together by one Edwin Otis North from West Allis, Wisconsin

Different strokes for different folks...

Approximately $38,000 and 3200 hours of labor have been put into Rick Dobbertin's twin-turbocharged, supercharged and nitrous oxide-injected 454-inch Pro Street Chevy Nova. Dobbertin is fortunate in that he owns a speed shop in Springfield, Virginia, and this complex piece of packaging represents a rolling billboard for that business (AA/Speed & Custom/Turbo Dynamics). The car has a full 2 × 3 in. rectangular tube frame featuring a fully removable front half, together with a 20-point internal roll cage. The front and rear suspension systems are comprised of 4-link split wishbones, a 6 in. dropped axle with Corvette spindles, home-built panhard rods, ladder bars, Koni shocks and four wheel disc brakes. Linking the twist from the monster motor to the 15 × 15 in. McCreary-wrapped Center Line wheels is a $34\frac{1}{2}$ in. wide Dana 60 rear end

Above The only thing sedate about this '65 sedan is its almost-stock sheet metal, painted in five shades of blue augmented by a silver base. All the original chrome trim—all 294 parts—is either new or re-plated. Rick visited no less than five states and eighteen Novas before he found a good-enough basis for this mind blowing project

Left The space shuttle has nothing on this! No less than seventeen Autometer gauges make up the imposing array

Overleaf Rick lets the parachutes loose on a lonely road, just to prove that this incredible machine actually runs
Overleaf inset Trunk is filled with such items as a nitrous system, polished aluminium fuel cell, a pair of batteries and two enormous wheeltubs

With huge 14 × 15 in. McCreary-shod Center Lines
under the bed and that super-tall powerplant, this little
hauler looks business-like from every angle. Jerry has
many friends to thank for helping him to get this machine
on the road in such a short time, not least his wife
Dorothy, who stitched up most of the interior trim

Paul Langley Jr has done what is laughingly known as *an engine transplant* in his little Renault Dauphine. He's not just doubled the capacity, not even quadrupled. No, he's dropped a mill in that it is very nearly *eight times* the size of the original. What started out.as an 845 cc rear-engined runabout is now a one-of-a-kind street machine with '59 Cadillac 390 ci power. The front seats have been moved back a couple of feet to make way for the engine, and Paul now looks out of the rear side window and enters the car by the rear door. It certainly is weird to see this car cruising the streets with, apparently, only a guy sitting in the back and no driver

Needless to say, the inside of this *Back Seat Driver* bears
no resemblance to the original Dauphine. The seats are
way back, the dash hand built, and the upholstery done
in red on black crushed velvet. Access to the back of the
engine is simply a matter of unscrewing the 'personalized'
bulkhead cover

Wide rims at either end of a stock-width Posi-Trak
Chevy axle gives a real cartoon look to the Renault's
rear. The old engine compartment is now luxuriously
upholstered with padded vinyl and deep pile carpeting
and it also houses a 16 gallon Ford fuel tank. Front
suspension, brakes and steering gear are Studebaker. The
owner is a body and fender man from Topeka, Kansas

It goes without saying that not every street enthusiast has the inclination or wherewithal to build a totally 'individual' machine. Many prefer to take a factory supercar from the by-gone era and restore it, maybe adding a few personal touches. Like the owner of this rare Judge Option Pontiac GTO, who went right through the stock 455 High Output engine before topping it off with a GMC blower and two 4-barrel carbs. Apart from the motor, this car is straight out of a 1971 Pontiac showroom

Overleaf In an effort to distinguish the new hi-performance Pontiac GTO from the basic model, a young engineer on the GTO committee suggested the name *The Judge* from the popular Rowan and Martin TV show *Laugh In*. It stuck, and just over 11,000 Judge Option GTOs were manufactured from 1969 to 1971. Of these, only 357 hardtops were sold in the final production year which explains why the owner has simply removed the hood and bolted on a supercharger. As an interesting aside, the head of that committee was one John Z. DeLorean who, it is quoted, 'created the GTO as a car for my own personal use . . .'

Being an assembly line worker at Ford's Rouge complex in Dearborn, Michigan, it's hardly surprising that Arthur Esper owns two Ford vehicles. One is a 302 Boss Mustang, currently under restoration, but the other is slightly *different*; this home-brewed 4 × 4 'English' Ford Thames panel truck. Arthur has successfully amalgamated the cute 1960 body with the all-wheel drive components from a '78 Jeep, thanks to a well-designed home-made frame. Not only that, but he's also managed to squeeze in a turbo'd 2-litre Pinto motor together with its 4-speed trans. A one-off adapter plate was needed to mate the latter with the 4-wheel drive transfer case. Arthur's neat little rig delivers a regular 27 mpg on the street but, and quote: 'It's really too good to take out in the woods'

Most off-beat 4-wheel drive combos are straightforward body swaps made to look as outrageous as possible with the addition of monster tyres. Arthur's Ford on the other hand has been tailor-made to look as if it came from the factory that way—disregarding the Candy Red custom paint job and Walt Disney-inspired artwork, of course

F-bodied flyers

Back in 1966, before production of General Motors new code-named F-car (GM's answer to Ford's new Mustang) had begun, the press had already labelled it the *Panther* and dies were even made up for the ornamentation of this name. However, at the last minute GM decided to call their new F-car *Camaro* which, as the publicists wrote, meant 'comrade, pal, buddy or friend' in French. It has proved to be a wise move. For three generations, the F-bodied Camaro and its subsequent derivative the Pontiac Firebird have been the most desirable friends that a sizeable segment of street machiners could wish to have. Long live the F-body!

First (background) and second generation F-bodies

It's amazing what a wild paint job and a new set of wheels can do for an otherwise plain '70 Camaro. This multi-hued SS396 appeared on the cover of *Hot Rod* in July 1980. Pro custom painter Bill Carter was the man with the patience

Custom paintwork on this '69 Super Sport Camaro is
early seventies style. Rear wheel-arch flares are 'out' too

First generation Z28s are now extremely collectible, and
this is one of only 602 that were built in 1967, the first
year of production. Candy-colored Camaro runs a
later-model 350-inch LT-1, another sought-after piece

Post-muscle era Z28 runs a heavy number up front and
you can be certain the owner likes to use it

A VW chassis is the best basis for any fibreglass fun car, whatever the shape!

Overleaf This '67 Camaro is one super-clean machine

Left and far left Richard Park and a few of his fellow street machiners from Sylvester, Georgia, put together this Pro Street Z28 in the eight weeks preceeding the Nationals. The boldly-striped vehicle features a real *Laurel'n'Hardy* wheel combination: 14 × 15s in the rear with 3½-inchers up front

Below Motivation is supplied by a supercharged 350 with low-compression pistons, Engle cam, Hooker headers and dual 600 Holley carbs. Slick ally panelling is *de rigeur* in a Pro Street engine compartment

Above and right George Matulik has given a new lease of life to an old '69 Camaro. What was a *hunkajunk* is now an eye-catching street machine with Ram Air 400 power and a velour interior. George hails from Bridgeview, Illinois

Left Pod-mounted tacho and other vital gauges ensures that George never has to take more than one eye off the road

Atlantic crossing

Above In Britain, the term 'street machine' is used more loosely to describe virtually any late-model vehicle that is *different* from the norm; be it mechanically, or as is more often the case, visually. A prime example is Richard Haskell's unique Jaguar, aptly nicknamed *Stray Cat*. Once a 4-door XJ saloon, the professional bodyman turned it into a 2-door XJ-S style coupe and sprayed it a deep shade of Candy Green. This labour-intensive project cost him just under £1000

Right The original rear doors have been welded 'shut', the roof sectioned, and the rear window metalwork moved forward by approximately 2 ft., creating a 2+2 seating arrangement. The extended bootlid is electrically operated, utilizing Mustang power hood rams

Left Six-wheeled Jaguar XJ-S pick-up was custom built as a promotional exercise for the *100 + International* wheel company. The 30 in. body and chassis extension carries a trailing IRS, while under the bonnet lies a 'built' eight cylinder 454 ci Chevy in place of the stock V12. Four cylinders less, but double the horsepower . . .

Above The *Interstate Six* Jag is a real attention-getter at shows

Overleaf Back in 1979 the landlord of *The Garricks* pub in Bristol, England, decided to build himself a special kind of beer bottle hauler which would also serve to bring in more custom. This 'home-brewed' '65 Daimler pick-up is the result of his inspiration. Once a $2\frac{1}{2}$ litre 4-door saloon, it's now equipped with a lightweight $3\frac{1}{2}$ litre Rover V8 and twin 'beer barrel' fuel tanks

Above Alan and his brother Trevor did all the work themselves over a period of three years, and that includes the two-tone Pearl paint job

Left Looking more like a Mustang fastback, Alan Bailey's radically altered '71 Capri is a good example of a show-winning British street machine. The high riding Ford from Gravesend in Kent features a fully chromed E type Jag rear end, beautifully detailed 327 Chevy motor and enough body modifications to fill a book

Overleaf At just 21, Andy Saunders from Poole in Dorset, is probably Britain's most prolific young customiser. Several of his machines have appeared in magazines and shows right across Europe, but so far none have been as popular as this; a '68 Volvo 121 hardtop turned fifties-style kustom convertible. Quite an achievement!

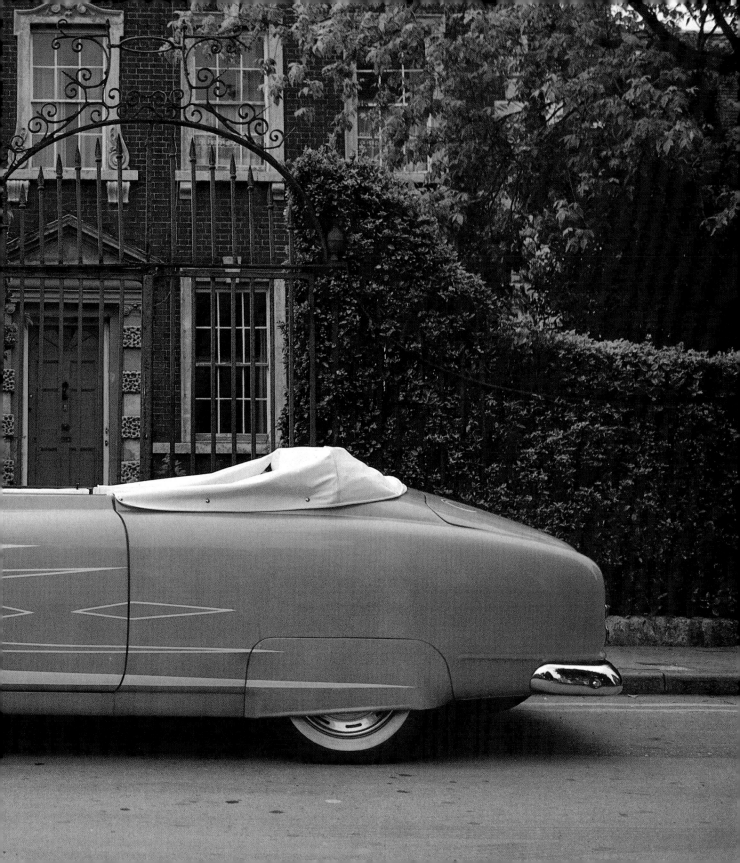

Right Front end mods include frenched headlights, rounded-off hood corners, and a much modified grille opening which incorporates a cut'n'shut '57 Vauxhall Victor front bumper. Neat

Below Not only was the roof chopped off, but the windshield pillars were sectioned too. This adds to the nostalgic flavour, especially when the white Carson-style top is up. Other traditional tricks include re-shaped rear fender tops and fender skirts, shaved door handles, a 4 in. lowering job on the suspension, polished Moon discs and Pearl paint. The 1800 motor is bone stock. This one's for 'show', not 'go'

This 'Mid Sussex Rodder' took an early Standard 10,
built a new chassis for it, and installed a Wade-blown
3-litre Ford V6 under a one-piece front end. Bright
yellow paint makes it a real stand-out at the Chelsea,
London cruise, held on the last Saturday of each month

Andy Saunders' latest creation; a '64 Austin Mini
shortened by 2 ft. 7 in. The car is known as *Mini Ha-Ha*
and it wheelstands in reverse!

Hobby horses

Way back in 1965, just after the famous ponycar had been
launched, FoMoCo's marketing division claimed that
'Mustangers have more fun!' The proud owner of this
California top-chopped, 428 Cobra Jet-powered '65
'Stang agrees wholeheartedly

Above and above right Grand Rapids, Michigan's David Jackson, rides herd on a 351 Boss. The original paint treatment of the '71 Mustang featured a black hood with a full-length black or silver side stripe, depending on the body color. Just to be different, David sprayed this heavy breathing horse a misty shade of blue with red hot flames

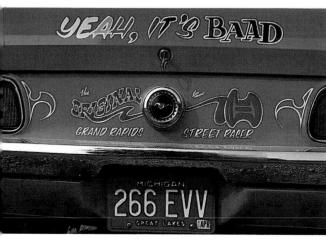

Left With high compression TRW pistons, Crower cam and an 800 cfm Holley, and a 5.14-geared Ford rear end, this is the view that most folks see most of

Above What better for a grocery-getter? 2-door station wagon from Ohio appeared at the '79 Machine Nats

Right Springfield residents get treated to an annual 3-day rolling car show—whether they like it or not! A Mustang II leads this particular line-up

Overleaf The 'Boss' era in Ford history came and went all too fast. It started in 1969 with the Boss 302 Mustang and ended in '72, the victim of government regulations and corporate politics. With a very potent, high-winding small block, the average Boss 302 ran 0 to 60 in around $6\frac{1}{2}$ seconds and clocked the $\frac{1}{4}$ mile in just under 15. It was a quick car, and there are still many people around who can appreciate its virtues. The owner of this re-painted 1970 model is one of 'em

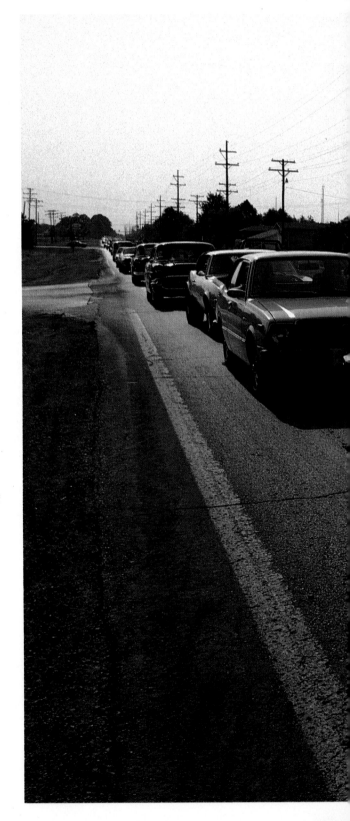

Pro Steed has a hot flame job and, moreover, enough 'oats'
under the hood to frighten off most would-be street
racers

Alston Engineering of Sacremento, California,
manufacture complete Pro Street chassis kits to fit all
Mustangs since 1965, including the late model fastback

Hot Vee-dubs

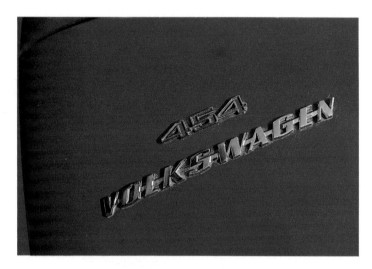

Above Think of the most outrageous possible modifications that can be made to a vehicle and you can almost guarantee that someone, somewhere has done it to the ubiquitous VW Bug. The very nature of the Volkswagen makes it the perfect basis for an individual creation, which is why there are so many truly unique VW street machines

Right Who'd ever suspect that underneath those molded-together front panels lies a 600 horsepower Chevy V8? Only the eagle-eyed would ever notice the radiator air intake between the front nerf bars. I'm sure. Had the owner refrained from striping the rear end of the car and kept the bodywork totally stock looking, this would have to be the ultimate sleeper (sheep in wolf's clothing)

'When I was a kid, my Dad told me that if you can't buy it, you build it.' So Arthur, Illinois' Bill Plank built it—all 460-inches of rat up front in a '69 VW! All his buddies said it couldn't be done, but Bill proved them wrong by designing and constructing a heavy-strength hot rod-style tube chassis which accepted the old beetle-shaped body and the 'new pieces'. These include a coil-sprung 12-bolt Chevy rear end and the complete front suspension from a Pontiac Firebird. The one-piece flip front was obviously a necessity

Jim Porter, a fishing tackle store owner from Springfield, Illinois, spent the best part of three years transforming a $100 '68 VW into this beautiful Baja Bug. While most Bajas are built to take the rough stuff, Jim built his to win trophies and to be seen on the street. In less than a year his efforts have been rewarded with over 20 pots at various shows, including those for *Best VW*, *Best Paint* and *People's Choice*. A cut-above the average 'People's Car', for sure!

For a car which had been abandoned on the freeway by its previous owner, this little Bug was in relatively good shape when Jim acquired it—apart from the usual badly-crunched fenders. Consequently, a 7-piece replacement Baja panel kit was the obvious route to take. In keeping with the underlying 'off-road' image the suspension has been raised, but those highly polished Center Line wheels and Goodyear tyres are strictly for the street. Other tricks include one-piece side windows, 1960 Corvette tail-lights, and of course that show-winning custom paint job, executed by pro painter Ernie Ball. Roughly six miles-worth of masking tape was said to be used in creating the multi-colored patterns. Starting with a gold base, the *Bad Bug* received varying amounts of Gold and Tangerine Candy followed by Purple, Blue and Dark Gold Murano—oh yes, with a little black lacquer in-between

Jim's flat four is so clean you could almost eat your dinner off it! Joe Grant and the boys at nearby *Off Road Supplies* assembled the mild 1679 cc engine, while the owner takes credit for all the fine detail work. Like the rest of the car it's built more for show, but that's not to say it wouldn't blow the doors off a stock VW . . .

Street Machine showcase

Above, right and overleaf Illinois truck owner/operator Lloyd McVey gets his kicks in this trendy '71 Dodge Challenger. Amongst other things it incorporates a complete Alston chassis and roll cage kit, a Strange Engineering-prepped Dana 60 rear end with ladder bars and Koni coil-over shocks, and a trick lift-off front end.

Power is supplied by a blown 426 ci Hemi which has been filled with go-faster goodies, like Arias pistons, Keith Black rods, crank and heads, and a Donovan valvetrain. The Dyers-driven supercharger is fed by a pair of Carter carbs and a Crager manifold. Only a fool would challenge this trucker

A no-nonsense 426 Stage III Wedge. Real muscle

Behind Chevrolet, Ford, Pontiac and Dodge, Plymouths
were the fifth most popular make of car at the Nationals.
Hot-rodded Road Runner was the meanest

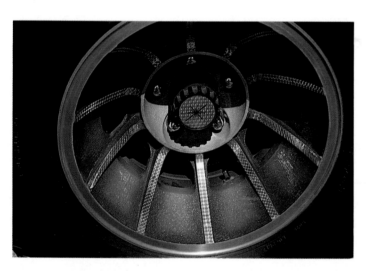

Above Who says you can't improve aftermarket wheels? This split vein-type has been given the two-color treatment to match the vehicle's bodywork. Diffraction tape adds that extra bit of sparkle

Right Crushed velvet door panel treatment was *nuthin'* compared to the fancy murals on the outside

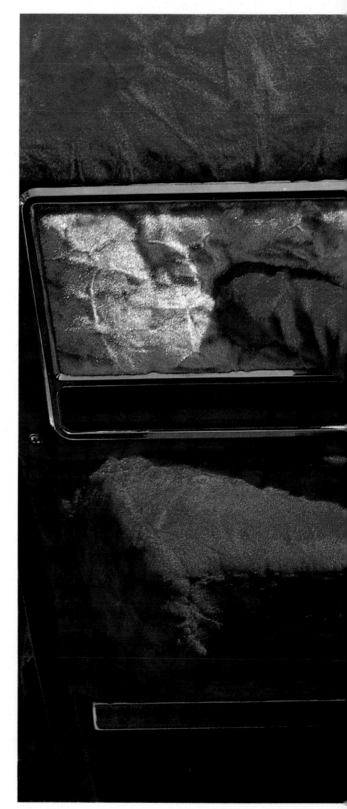

Danny Taylor's '79 Malibu is late-model customising at
its best. The candy-colored masterpiece from Louisville,
Kentucky, has been top-chopped 5 in., liberally louvered,
dechromed, and boasts a full hydraulic suspension
system enabling the owner to alter the ride height at the
flick of a switch. The tube grille, bumpers and tinted
windows weren't issued at the factory, and neither was a
black crushed velvet interior. Built as something of a
promo vehicle for the family body 'n' paint business, this
low-down Chevy steals the show wherever it goes

Extraordinary Isetta made a lot of folks smile at the 1979
Street Machine Nationals in Milwaukee. Hanging out
back is a 110 hp flat six Chevy Corvair engine!

Dave Russell decided on a hogged-out 350 small block to power his flip-front '72 Vega. Carburation is supplied by a trio of gold-tipped Webers on an Offenhauser manifold

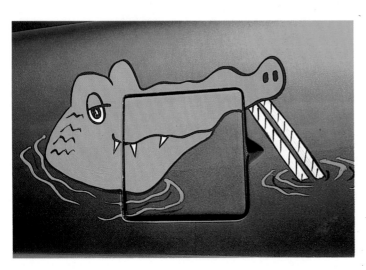

Above Hand-painted artwork on a '56 Chevy filler door was probably inspired by a gas-guzzling motor at the other end

Right Big bad blown Chevelle is a typical late sixties/early seventies street machine—guaranteed to send a shiver up the local sherrif's spine!

Left The average age of the 5000 participants at the 1983 Street Machine Nationals was 25.3 years, and over half of them drove Chevies. The Nationals is very much a male-orientated event

Overleaf The flanks of this lean machine are 'cobwebbed'; an age-old custom paint technique whereby long, stringy blobs of paint are spat out of the spraygun at very low pressure

Right The St. Louis-based Biscayne carries some fine pinstriping and paint changes, as well as 427 muscle power up front

Below One sure-fire way to do a wheelie is to move the rear axle forward a couple of feet, like Dan Virga's '68 Chevy Biscayne. He calls it *Overhang* for the obvious reason

Left The sound of the wheezer on this stock-bodied late model must raise a few eyebrows down at the local shopping center

Above No street machine book would be complete without a shot of the classic '57 Chevy. This old-fashioned street racer is unusual in that it's a rag top, although the sixties 'backyard hot rod' touches are all there. The SS 396 grille badge signifies what's behind it

Danny Ramsey's '67 Chevy Nova has all the attributes of
the contemporary Pro Street movement: eye-catching
paint, awesome tyres and wheels, the appropriate
bodscoop and plenty of muscle (468 Chevy) to back it
all up. Ramsey built the entire car single-handed and won
the coveted *1st Place Pro Street* award at the 1982 *Car
Craft* Nats—when he was just 18! He is now the sole
proprietor of Dan Ramsey Race Cars, located in Porter,
Indiana

Above Blacked-out 1970 Pro Street Nova is just too *baad*!

Left Heavy Chevies

A convertible Impala would be most folks idea of fun on a
warm summer's evening, but some still prefer *CRUZIN*
in a roll-caged GTO

No shame if you didn't recognise this eight headlight
wonder as being a '74 Olds Cutlass; it's been sectioned
3 in., chopped 4 in., and lowered 5 in. There has also
been about 10 in. taken out of the length, where the
back seat was. Owner Bob Peterson has put some really
neat tricks into his black'n'flamed custom, including
electric windows, door locks, trunk lid, and even a
flip-down front licence plate

Below Steve and Kari Pierce show their clean green '66 Ford Thunderbird as often as possible

Right One way of keeping cool in the hot and dusty atmosphere of the Street Machine Nationals is to cruise the fairgrounds in a blown Chevelle

This street freak was just a harmless Ford Falcon before
'Vito's Garage' got hold of it

Most street machines, like Camaros and Mustangs, begin life as factory performance cars whose very presence seems to scream muscle. The Ford Fairmont on the other hand was designed to transport the average American motorist in comfort, style and grace—which is exactly why *Car Craft* magazine transformed this one and gave it away as a grand prize at their '81 Machine Nationals. It proves that almost any kind of vehicle with four wheels is fair game for street machiners